Meet Me for COFFEE

Art by Frankie Buckley

TEXT BY

Holly Halverson
Beryl Peters
Dave Davidson

Harvest House Publishers
Eugene, Oregon

Copyright ©1998 Harvest House Publishers, Eugene, Oregon 97402

Library of Congress Cataloging-in-Publication Data
Meet me for Coffee / Illustrated By Frankie Buckley
        p.   cm.
      ISBN 1-56507-661-3
      1. Coffee—Quotations, maxims, etc.
TX415.M44   1997
641.3373—dc21

97-8312
CIP

Buckley Studio
35 The Hillside
Stringer, MS 39481
(601) 649-1759

Some text used in this volume was originally published in *Etiquette for Coffee Lovers* ©Beryl Peters,
published by Copper Beech Publishing Ltd., East Grinstead Sussex England RH19 4FS.
Used by agreement.

Design and production by Left Coast Design, Portland, Oregon

Scripture quotations are from The Living Bible, Copyright ©1971 owned by assignment
by Illinois Regional Bank N.A. (as trustee). Used by permission of Tyndale
House Publishers, Inc., Wheaton, Illinois 60189.

Contents

Introduction

The very smell of fresh coffee can make the mouth water as it summons up the warmth of the early morning's first drink, the mid-morning break, the busy lunchtime and the after-dinner luxury.

BERYL PETERS

very coffee connoisseur knows: coffee is more than a drink. It's more than liquid refreshment useful for washing down after-dinner cookies and breakfast Danish. It's more than a staple you keep in constant supply, like flour and sugar. Coffee is even more than the sum of its parts: a hearty, rich scent; a steaming, frothy fluid; a purveyor of reassuring percolating sounds; a pleasing, warm brew that slides down so soothingly.

The millions who enjoy it as part of their daily grind know coffee is a companion, though an inanimate one. Coffee goes along on trips, opens a conversation, closes a meal, invites fellowship, initiates romance, accompanies work hours, and helps heal the fractures of a day. Coffee isn't just something we drink as a side item; it's often the

Coffee helps us rise to challenges, overcome hurdles, and, at the end of the day, savor our victories.

BENJAMIN FRANKLIN

main course, the reason for our meeting, the day's finest moment. It's something we count on as much (or more often) than a close friend. Coffee bridges the routines, interruptions, joys, and surprises of our days, and many of us would say it helps us glide through them more gracefully.

So go ahead—pull out a fresh cup. Fill it to the rim. Taste it with all your senses. And share some with a friend who needs it.

Part of the appeal of coffee is that it is a drink that marks the transitions in our day . . . from sleeping to waking, from work to rest, from day to night. . . . It accompanies us through the day like a talisman of both change and continuity.

CAROLYN MILLER

DARK ROASTED Coffee BEANS

Hazelnut BEANS

GRANDMA'S TEACAKES

W N S E

Frankie Buckley ©

Sweetening one's coffee is generally the first stirring event of the day.
EVAN ESAR

The Quiet Exclamation Mark

It's true that coffee often serves as punctuation. It stops, starts, helps us continue through the events of the day. It's an essential at dawn's breakfast, an anticipated refresher between tasks, the pick-me-up at noon, the late-day gentle jolt, and the savory elixir that celebrates the coming of dusk. Coffee, you see, gives us a quiet exclamation mark when we need it. When that project is complete, the file closed, our energy exhausted, we need it as a reward for a job well (and finally!) done—or as a friendly prod to start again.

All of us know someone who won't speak until she has her "cup of joe" firmly in hand. It

I've set personal conditions, reserving my coffee drinking for special occasions such as walking into the kitchen.
HUGH MYRRH

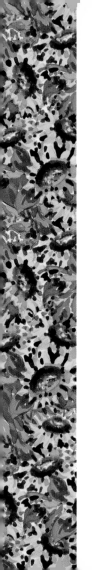

helps form her first sentence of the day, and no discernible utterances precede it. Pity the man, woman, or child who tries to provoke conversation before the pot is on. But once coffee has hit its mark, the eyes widen, the lips unlock, and the thoughts fly. Who of us really wants to start a car without keys? Coffee is so much easier to keep track of; it's always in the same place.

We would feign deny ourselves the satisfaction, either, of putting a period at the end of the day with a hearty toast over an exquisite brew made from freshly ground, luxuriously scented, deep-brown beans. Dessert isn't really necessary when you have this to sip, but bitter and sweet have always been buddies. Why not? A bit of cake, a slice of pie, a cup of fruit crisp could only enhance this final sigh of the evening.

And all the in-between times—the quick chat with a neighbor, the visit with an aunt, the greeting of a colleague, the communing with a client—call for a medium of friendly exchange. Coffee always suits. Coffee encourages conversation. Coffee invites the jovial, attracts the formal, affirms the casual. Coffee fits everywhere and anywhere.

Whether you're starting or finishing, taking a short breather or a permanent break, keep coffee close by to set the tone. It marks any moment with affable punch and welcome warmth.

I have known the evening, morning and afternoon.
. . . I have measured my life in coffee spoons.

T.S. ELIOT

THE STORY OF COFFEE

The stories and mysteries surrounding this drink show what an important and valuable commodity coffee has been over the centuries. Even the origin of its name is in doubt. Some say the word *coffee* comes from:

KAWECH
an Arabic word meaning strength and vigor

KAHWEH
from the Turks, meaning "exciting"

KAFFA
a province of Ethiopia

THE STORY OF STARVATION ...
One story says that an exiled Arabian Sheik saved himself from starvation in the wilderness by making soup from the berries of the coffee shrub.

THE STORY OF THE GOAT HERDER …

Another tale tells us that Kaldi, a goat herder, observing the frolicsome behavior of his goats after they had eaten the fruit of the coffee tree, prepared some for himself in the form of a beverage. He and his dervishes so appreciated this new drink that they drank it at night in order to keep awake during their vigils. The goat herder introduced it to the monks in the nearby monastery, and it worked on them too, keeping them awake during their long hours of prayer!

TRYING TO KEEP THE SECRET …

As early as the twelfth century, the Arab countries were cultivating the coffee plant. Those who knew about coffee did not, however, want to share their good fortune.

Coffee had first arrived in Arabia from Ethiopia or West Africa around 600 A.D. Coffee soon spread through the entire Middle East, and they were fanatical about not letting the secret of its cultivation out, so they restricted its circulation. For many years they refused to let coffee beans leave the country unless they had been cooked or dried to prevent the use of the seed germ by others.

THE SECRET'S OUT …

By 1500 the Turks had introduced coffee to Eastern Europe, which they ruled. Vienna and Paris soon took to drinking

coffee, and it spread to Britain. The Dutch took the bean to Ceylon and to the East Indies, and eventually the coffee plant was introduced to Brazil, where it was established over a quarter of the country.

AND FINALLY, IN AMERICA…

Our forefathers and mothers favored coffee, shunning the drinking of tea because of the enormous import taxes being charged on it.

In 1773, at the Boston Tea Party, locals showed what they thought of Britain by dressing up as Indians, sneaking aboard British merchant ships docked in the harbor, and throwing the expensive cargo overboard. They then drank coffee all the more as an act of defiance!

A SELECTED TIME LINE

600	*Beans first discovered*
1100	*Plants cultivated in Arabia*
1635	*First coffee hits Oxford, England*
1663	*Milk is added in Holland to lessen bitterness*
1770	*Coffee develops into a worldwide commodity*
1903	*Caffeine-free coffee developed in America*
1950	*Espresso machines become more popular*
1997	*Approximately 1,800 new coffee stores open in the U.S.*

The morning cup of coffee has an exhilaration about it which the cheering influence of the afternoon or evening cup of tea cannot be expected to reproduce.

OLIVER WENDELL HOLMES

This Ain't Tea!

Much ado is made over a soothing cup of tea served in a delicate, hand-painted cup. The dainties that fortify tea time— scones, watercress sandwiches, trifle—are light fare served in small portions, and intentionally so. Tea parties are occasions for one's best manners, dressiest attire, smallest appetite, and lowest voice.

Don't misunderstand. Tea has its place, and its own measure of comfort. Coffee is just, well, thicker. Heartier. Coffee inspires loud laughter as well as whispered

I like it as thick as oil and dark as a world with the sun shot out.

MAY BLUE

17

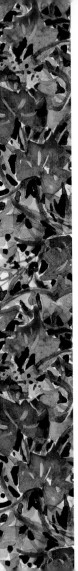

secrets. Coffee can be enjoyed by someone wearing flannel as well as someone wearing lace. Formalities aside, long words abandoned, reserve dropped: Coffee invites the you *you* really are.

No wonder coffee is the first beverage offered to unexpected company. When coffee is the centerpiece of a gathering, no embossed invitations or RSVPs are required to document the occasion. And coffee rarely has more intricate instructions than just carefully measuring water and grounds; that opulent aroma comes as easy as pie (and smells just that good)—no steeping, squeezing limp bags, or removal of leaves necessary.

The conversation that arises over the enveloping steam can be as carefree as "How was your day?" or as deep as "I'm so sorry you had to go through that." A constantly refilled mug communicates that time is available; you can say all you need to; you'll be heard. You can leave the trivial at the door and bring your heart to the table, if you need to.

If morsels are more to your liking, stick to tea. If it's meaty meetings you're after, coffee's your choice. It seems the world has made its preference known: Ever seen a tea receptacle the size of a cappuccino cup?

The last proof that coffee or tea is favourable to intellectual expression is that all nations use one or the other as aids to conversation.

PHILIP G. HAMERTON

TURKISH COFFEE

Coffee from Mocha is used for Turkish coffee. The grounds are pulverized, and it is made in an "Ibrik"—a traditional long-handled copper pan. After the coffee has been brought to a boil three times using equivalent amounts of coffee and sugar and only a small amount of water, it is left to stand for a few minutes to let the grounds settle. The coffee is served in small cups, which are never filled to the brim. Filled cups are a sign of disrespect.

ESPRESSO

Espresso coffee is a distinctive dark, strong coffee that is favored in Italy. It is made by forcing steam through the finely ground, dark roasted beans. Espresso is drunk in smaller quantities and is slightly

bitter and thick. Before World War II, the Italians were injecting steam through coffee to make espresso, and shortly afterward they invented the espresso machines.

CAPPUCCINO

This hot, frothy, milky coffee is espresso with extras and was one of Italy's favorite drinks, which spread throughout Europe in the 1950s. It got its name because its soft-brown color resembled the robes of the

Capuchin order of monks! Cappuccino soon became a worldwide favorite with the addition of whipped cream, cinnamon, cocoa powder, or flaked chocolate.

Is there a better blend than good coffee with a best friend?
In the coffee cup of life, friends are the sugar cubes.

DAVE DAVIDSON

A Few of My Favorite Words

In the chaos, a phone rings. A beep signals you have new e-mail. Or the fax machine scrolls out a message: *Meet me for coffee.* A sigh of relief escapes your lips as you grab a jacket and head, without hesitation, to an understood destination. There you settle in your usual place and await your friend's arrival. You wonder what to order today: latte? Something stronger— a shot of espresso mellowed by a bit of cream? Maybe your inner thermostat indicates you need cooling off, so you mull over iced coffee options. No

Every good thing multiplies when it is shared by two with the same heart.

HEATHER KOPP

21

matter what you choose, just sitting there amongst the delicious scents and fellow imbibers lulls you to a more peaceful place than the one you left.

Members of the local coffee klatch, at home or in the office, have given themselves a new name: "Sisters of the Bean." A well-rounded break time calls for more than agile jaws and a comfortable meeting spot; partakers must gather round more than common ground. A common grind—espresso, cappuccino, raspberry, German chocolate, cinnamon—makes for livelier discourse and lighter moods. This is, perhaps, coffee's finest contribution, that of creating companionable ambiance that draws folk of like mind and similar situations into discussion. Sisters of the Bean (Brothers, too) share a camaraderie that runs deep: They meet often (coffee is a daily, if not hourly, habit), appreciate the way warm Java makes words flow, and they keep both running freely. The result is nothing less than stronger friendship, deeper understanding, and firmer emotional footing.

It's unknown exactly how coffee evolved to its current hallowed state, but it's easy to see how it keeps its place of honor. Coffee is our favorite excuse for coming together and our favorite reason for staying a little longer. "A fresh pot, you say? All right. I'll have another cup. Biscotti? Sure, I'll try some."

Whose phone, fax, or e-mail can you ring today with those much-anticipated words: "Meet me for coffee!"

The very best form of office communication is not e-mail,
a fax, or a memo. It's the coffee break!

DAVE DAVIDSON

When the coffee is hot,
And the talk is good,
And the feeling is easy,
And the memories are many,
But the time is too short—
You know you're with a friend.

AUTHOR UNKNOWN

Coffee Bread

1 pound flour
1 teaspoon salt
1½ ounces sugar
2 ounces butter

approximately ½ pint milk
2 fresh eggs
2 teaspoons baking powder

Put three quarters of the flour into a mixing bowl, heat it until warm to the touch, and add the salt and sugar. Put the butter and milk into a saucepan, and stir until warm and well mixed. Make a well in the center of the flour, add the warm milk and butter gradually, forming into a smooth batter. Add eggs and beat well. Mix the baking powder with the remaining flour, and add this quickly to the batter at the last moment. Fill greased bread pans half full, and bake in a hot oven for 20 minutes. Serve with fresh coffee.

Coffee Fritters

Cut three milk rolls into even-sized pieces, about ¼ inch thick, and remove the crust. Put the slices in a pie pan, and pour over them about ½ pint of strong, clear coffee, flavored with a few drops of vanilla essence. When the bread has absorbed the liquid, but before it has become pulpy, dip the pieces into a thick pancake batter, so as to cover them completely. Fry them golden brown in hot fat. Drain and cover well with sugar and a little ground cinnamon.

Coffee Dream Cake

2 ¼ cups cake flour
1 ½ cups sugar
1 tablespoon baking powder
1 teaspoon salt
¾ cup *strong* black coffee

6 eggs, separated
¼ cup butter, melted
1 teaspoon vanilla
2 egg whites
1 tablespoon confectioner's sugar

Preheat oven to 325°. Sift together flour, ¾ cup sugar, baking powder, and salt. Add coffee, egg yolks, butter, and vanilla. Blend until smooth. In a separate large bowl, beat all egg whites until they peak. Gradually beat in remaining ¾ cup sugar. Fold egg whites into batter. Pour batter into ungreased 10-inch tube pan. Bake 1 hour. Invert cake and cool completely. Sprinkle with confectioner's sugar.

Chocolate Mayonnaise Cake

1 package (18 ¾ ounces)
  chocolate cake mix—
  the kind with pudding in the mix
½ cup Hershey's cocoa

3 eggs
1 cup mayonnaise
1 ⅓ cups water

Preheat oven to 350°.
Grease and flour two 9-inch pans.
With mixer on lowest speed,
combine together dry cake mix
and cocoa in large bowl. Add
remaining ingredients and beat
just until blended. Beat at medium
speed for two minutes. Pour into
pans. Bake for 30–35 minutes, or
until cake tester inserted in center comes out clean. Cool in pans
for 10 minutes. Remove and completely cool on racks.

Frosting:
1 package (4 ounces) vanilla
  instant pudding
¾ cup confectioner's sugar
1 cup cold milk
1 container (8 ounces) Cool Whip

Combine pudding and sugar;
add milk. Mix with rotary beater
until well-blended and smooth.
Let stand for 5 minutes. Fold in
whipped topping. Spread on cake
at once. (Leftover cake should be
refrigerated or frosting will melt.)

Coffee Pudding

5 ounces fine bread crumbs
2 ounces of candied peel
$\frac{1}{2}$ pint coffee
3 ounces golden raisins

3 ounces sugar
2 eggs
grated rind of 1 lemon
$\frac{1}{4}$ pint milk

Put the bread in a mixing bowl with the candied peel, the grated lemon rind, the raisins, and sugar. Whisk the eggs, and add to them the milk and coffee. Stir into the dry ingredients. When well mixed, let stand for 10 minutes, then pour into a greased mold and bake in a moderate oven.

The power of this incredi-brew is almost too great to conceive.
Through morning, noon, and night, it will help you achieve.

BENJAMIN FRANKLIN

Just What the Doctor Ordered

oredom. Inertia. Writer's Block. Painter's Block. My Particular Block—yours, too. We know the handiest cure is as close as the kitchen counter. All we need to set this lethargy packing is a good stiff cup of joe . . . and history backs our theory.

We're told Beethoven counted out sixty beans for every cup of coffee he consumed—and look at the artistic result! Honore de Balzac credited his abundant writing career to prolific coffee consumption. Sebastian Bach declared his profound affection

Call it Java, bean drink,
roasted-black water, the
writer's drug, steamin' tar,
roasted caffeine or coffee,
just make sure it's in a cup
near my bed when I awake.

NELSON LIN

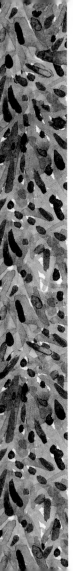

for the daily grind by saying, "Coffee is sweeter than honey, better than a thousand [yes, a thousand] kisses." Reportedly Napoleon avoided wine, but imbibed coffee throughout the day, "to revive the spirits and invigorate the body." An abundance of the beany brew kept German poet Goethe in a state of near-delirium as he was writing *The Sorrows of Werter*. A cup of caffeine uncorked the talents of Picasso, Van Gogh, and Monet. And apparently Lady Astor found courage in the cup to say to Winston Churchill: "If you were my husband, I'd put poison in your coffee." To which he, similarly inspired, replied, "If you were my wife, I'd drink it."

So it goes, down through the years, coffee's loosing talents, often to marvelous and time-honored results. Is it any surprise? Who of us hasn't appreciated the fresh vista we see after drinking a reviving cup, both deep and wide, of the rich brown river? Why do so many of us set our coffee machines to start perking at the same moment we start stirring? Why are coffee mugs—no other beverage vessel can boast this—available in designs specially constructed for travel? And note the varied forms it takes to satisfy mass appeal: You don't just have to drink it. You can chew chocolate-covered espresso beans or savor its flavor in cheesecake. The warm hum of coffee enlivens angel food cake and puts the bite in ice cream. You need never look far for a coffee buzz—it's everywhere.

Our favored antidote for boredom and its tiresome relatives is but a few steps away. Take some now.

> *Strong coffee, much strong coffee, is what awakens me.*
> *Coffee gives me warmth, waking, an unusual force and a*
> *pain that is not without very great pleasure.*

NAPOLEON

Coffee falls into the stomach . . . ideas begin to move, things remembered arrive at full gallop . . . the shafts of wit start up like sharp-shooters, similies arise, the paper is covered with ink.

HONORE DE BALZAC

HINTS FOR THE BEST COFFEE IN THE WORLD 1887

I t requires merely care and common sense to make the best coffee in the world:

1 Those who have the means of roasting coffee beans should always buy them unroasted.

2 There are machines for roasting coffee, but the best way is in the frying pan. The beans should be placed in the pan over a fire; stir gently until they are a dark mahogany color. Take them off the fire and allow to cool.

3 They should be ground as soon as cool. Use a coffee mill, and do not let the grocer grind them for you as you do not know how long they have been ground.

4 When the beans are roasted, they should always be kept in an air-tight receptacle, the best form being wide-necked bottles with glass stoppers.

5 As soon as the coffee is ground, boiling water should be poured upon it, and it should be left near the fire for a few minutes before pouring it out gently.

6 It can be strained through a fine filter or flannel bag into the coffee pot for the breakfast table.

A passionate new romance and fresh coffee have a lot in common. Both make the heart beat a bit faster.

DAN DAVIDSON

Love Among the Beans

The nineties have witnessed a switching of affections. Men and women on dates used to hold court in theaters, fancy restaurants, or dance clubs. Though all those establishments still enjoy active business, the coffee house has earned the allegiance of those experimenting with romance for the first (or fortieth) time. Why? Because "Want to get some coffee?" is so casual an invitation, so uninhibited a request, so unthreatening a premise that no one can refuse. What better way to explore the tastes and dreams of a potential

Oh, lover and beloved, eat and drink! Yes, drink deeply!

THE SONG OF SOLOMON

37

partner than by exchanging thoughts and glances over cups of shyly ordered and subtly enjoyed dark nectar?

The ambiance of the coffee house—the mingling voices, fragrant aromas, delectable desserts—encourages relaxed manner and calm collusion. Friendship rises naturally, like steam from the cups, and words drop between sips in an easy current. Romance can find roots here; this is fertile ground.

For those already ensconced in romantic bliss or those just testing the concept, coffee drinking provides an arena where words and emotions find expression. (Espresso makes for quicker commitments and more robust declarations of devotion.) How many spouses have soothed an aching head with the suggestion they go out for coffee after dinner? Can we count the engagements forged over flavored creams, the hands that entwined over the plate of almond biscotti? How many a suitor has been spied from across the room, the reasoning being "If he likes coffee, he must be all right."

It's true no statistics exist to prove coffee's influence on those tending toward love, but one thing is sure: All that fluid conversation can't hurt.

He was overwhelmed with a passion for chance, for making a move,
not to lose sight of this girl; off he darted from his chair.
With a voice he never knew he possessed he called out to her.
"Miss, you need coffee?" . . . "Miss," he meant to say,
"you need coffee, you need to let me know you, you need to sit
at my table and let me memorize those incredible eyes."

BECCA LYNN

It was a pleasant café warm and clean and friendly,
and I hung up my old water proof on the coat rack to dry
and put my worn and weathered felt hat on the rack
above the bench and ordered a café au lait. The waiter
brought it and I took out a notebook from my pocket
of the coat and a pencil and I began to write.

ERNEST HEMINGWAY

COFFEE HOUSES

In the early days of coffee, it was difficult for the average person to make the brew successfully. The whole process was cloaked in mystery.

There soon appeared a variety of coffee houses where ordinary people could go to buy a cup of ready-prepared coffee, and a club atmosphere developed around the drinking places. It seems that no matter where these coffee houses were established, they had at least one thing in common—women were barred!

In the first half of the nineteenth century in England, often the only place for any refreshment away from home was the pub. Campaigners for temperance, like John Wesley, saw the need for nonalcoholic drinks to be served in places similar to the pub. "British Workmen" establishments offered a similar atmosphere to the pubs, but with coffee as the drink rather than strong alcohol.

The Coffee Palace of East London was opened in 1873; then came the People's Cafes in 1874. These new coffee houses offered good cheap food and clean surroundings. Before this, there hadn't been respectable places for mom and the children to have a cup of coffee or a midday meal.

These cafes were the forerunners of modern-day coffee and tea shops—those delightful places where the drinks are hot and the friendships warm.

It is said that our custom of tipping arose from the coffee house days when patrons had to place money in a box marked T.I.P.—in order To Insure Promptness.

It's a lot more than just a drink; it's something happening.
Not as in hip, but like an event, a place to be,
but not like a location, but like somewhere within yourself.
It gives you time, but not actual hours or minutes,
but a chance to be, like be yourself, and have a second cup.

GERTRUDE STEIN

Alone with a Cup

One is never completely alone when a cup of coffee rests at her elbow. When human companions can't be found, that big friendly cup, a gift from one of those chums, stands in their stead, urging introspection. Thoughts swirl in a mellow fashion, much like the cream in her brew. There is no hurry here, no anxious thought. This is just the time to reflect and savor the marvel of beans ground to a powder and mixed with clear water.

The solitude sipper might look out a window as she muses, or she might not. Outdoor scenery is less

> *There is something undeniably heartwarming in a cup . . . . It is an ideal prescription for banishing loneliness.*
>
> **1921 BOOK OF ETIQUETTTE**

important than her inner landscape for these moments. There she explores the hills and valleys of her day or week or year; she chooses the next paths she'll take. She contemplates the faces that people her world and gives thanks appropriately. She wishes for more times like these and celebrates this unexpected pleasure by having another cup.

The role coffee plays in such a scene is subtle but not passive. As the only other warm body in the room, it comforts as it refreshes. Although it can't stimulate conversation or offer advice, it can by its unobtrusiveness summon soothing to a weary person. It can be the first step toward rest and a conclusion that *More of this is exactly what I need.*

Relaxing is only the start. It's what the consumer and her coffee do with the other hours that makes the difference in life. As coffee's creative juices flow, the drinker's dreams may awaken. Purpose may be restored. Ideas may hatch. Bitterness may break and forgiveness be extended ... all from a few minutes alone with a coffee cup.

When a friend isn't available, a cup of coffee always is. Spend liberal time with each.

When I'm alone with my thoughts, whether reading a book or writing a letter, coffee closes out distractions, enhancing the mood like a canopy companion of serene solitude.

JENNI NELSON

Heavenly Coffee

1 cup instant coffee
1 ½ cups powdered milk
½ teaspoon nutmeg
2 cups non-dairy creamer

⅔ to ¾ cup sugar (or use 18
    packages of sweetner)
2 teaspoons cinnamon
1 to 2 individual packets
    of hot chocolate mix

Mix all ingredients thoroughly. Use 2 to 3 teaspoons per cup of hot water. Smells heavenly and tastes even better!

Conclusion

Coffee is the common man's gold, and like gold,
it brings to every man the feeling of luxury and nobility.

ABD-AL-KADIR

Coffee, as we've seen, fits many moods and every occasion. It draws folks together, eases conversation, and bonds strangers into community. It's the friend that's always at hand, the jump-start for exhaustion, and the heartiest toast to the day's end.

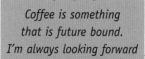

Coffee has accompanied some of our greatest artists and keenest minds. It's sparked brilliant ideas. It's succored the cold in heart and weary of mind. It's brightened the eyes, quickened the speech, and nurtured the development of dreams.

Coffee is something
that is future bound.
I'm always looking forward
to the next cup.

R. TILLAMOOK

What more could we ask of such a simple beverage? Only that another cup is poured…and another…and another….

Espresso, cappuccino, whatever it may be . . .
Moments shared with you,
the perfect place for me.

Wishing you many moments
of caffeinated pleasure.